23	24	25	26	27	28	29	30
50.942	51.996	54.938	55.845	58.933	58.693	63.546	65.39
Vanadium	Chromium	Manganese	Iron	Cobalt	Nickel	Cooper	Zinc

41	42					47	48
Nb	**M**					**Ag**	**Cd**
92.906						107.87	112.41
Niobium	Moly					Niobium	Niobium

73	74					79	80
Ta						**Au**	**Hg**
180.95						196.97	200.59
Tantalum						Gold	Mercury

105	106					111	112
Db	**S**					**Uuu**	**Uub**

92

Uranium

MC

Mason Crest

92

Uranium

By Jane P. Gardner

Mason Crest

450 Parkway Drive, Suite D
Broomall, PA 19008
www.masoncrest.com

Printed and bound in the United States of America.

Series ISBN: 978-1-4222-3837-0
Hardback ISBN: 978-1-4222-3847-9
EBook ISBN: 978-1-4222-7952-6

First printing
1 3 5 7 9 8 6 4 2

Produced by Shoreline Publishing Group LLC
Santa Barbara, California
Editorial Director: James Buckley Jr.
Designer: Patty Kelley
www.shorelinepublishing.com

Library of Congress Cataloging-in-Publication Data on file with the Publisher.

Cover photographs by Warut Roongathai/Wikimedia (left); Department of Defense (center); Riccochet69/Dreamstime.com; Holyworks/Dreamstime.com (bkgd).

QR Codes disclaimer:

You may gain access to certain third party content ("Third-Party Sites") by scanning and using the QR Codes that appear in this publication (the "QR Codes"). We do not operate or control in any respect any information, products, or services on such Third-Party Sites linked to by us via the QR Codes included in this publication, and we assume no responsibility for any materials you may access using the QR Codes. Your use of the QR Codes may be subject to terms, limitations, or restrictions set forth in the applicable terms of use or otherwise established by the owners of the Third-Party Sites. Our linking to such Third-Party Sites via the QR Codes does not imply an endorsement or sponsorship of such Third-Party Sites, or the information, products, or services offered on or through the Third-Party Sites, nor does it imply an endorsement or sponsorship of this publication by the owners of such Third-Party Sites.

Uranium

KEY ICONS TO LOOK FOR

Words to Understand: These words with their easy-to-understand definitions will increase the reader's understanding of the text, while building vocabulary skills.

Sidebars: This boxed material within the main text allows readers to build knowledge, gain insights, explore possibilities, and broaden their perspectives by weaving together additional information to provide realistic and holistic perspectives.

Educational Videos: Readers can view videos by scanning our QR codes, providing them with additional educational content to supplement the text. Examples include news coverage, moments in history, speeches, iconic moments, and much more!

Text-Dependent Questions: These questions send the reader back to the text for more careful attention to the evidence presented here.

Research Projects: Readers are pointed toward areas of further inquiry connected to each chapter. Suggestions are provided for projects that encourage deeper research and analysis.

Series Glossary of Key Terms: This back-of-the-book glossary contains terminology used throughout this series. Words found here increase the reader's ability to read and comprehend higher-level books and articles in this field.

Introduction

Take a close look around you. What do you see? A wall, a cat, a book, yesterday's lunch dishes. Outside your window, you might see clouds or rain or the sun shining while your heart pumps your blood throughout your body. All of those things, the solids, liquids, and gases around you, are composed of elements of the periodic table.

The periodic table is an arrangement of all the naturally occurring, and manufactured, elements known to humans at this point in time. There are 92 elements that can be found naturally on Earth and in space. The remaining 26 (and counting) have

WORDS TO UNDERSTAND

isotope   an atom of a specific element that has a different number of neutrons; it has the same atomic number but a different atomic mass

No matter where you go, elements make up everything you see around you.

been manufactured and analyzed in a lab. These elements, alone or in combination with others, form and shape all the matter around us. From the air we breathe, to the water we drink, to the food we eat—all these things are made of elements.

A lot of information about an element can be learned just by finding its location on the periodic table. The periodic table has undergone several updates and reorganizations since it was first developed in 1869. The modern version of the table used today is arranged by increasing atomic number into rows and columns. Each element has a unique atomic number. It is the number of protons in the nucleus of the atom. For example, uranium has an atomic number of 92—there

Uranium

are 92 protons in the nucleus. Hydrogen, on the other hand, has only one. All samples of an element have the same number of protons, but they may have a different number of neutrons in the nucleus. Atoms with the same number of protons but different number of neutrons are called **isotopes**. Certain chemical properties can be interpreted based on which group or row an element resides in. Each element on the periodic table is unique, having its own chemical and physical properties. The periodic table also gives important information such as the number of protons and neutrons in the nucleus of one atom of an element, the number of electrons that surround the nucleus, the atomic mass, and the general size of the atom. It is also possible to predict which state of matter an element is designated by a chemical symbol—a one- or two- (or

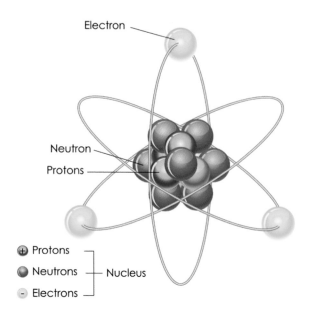

Electron

Neutron

Protons

⊕ Protons
● Neutrons — Nucleus
⊖ Electrons

Diagrams like this one show how electrons spin around an atom's nucleus.

Periodic Table

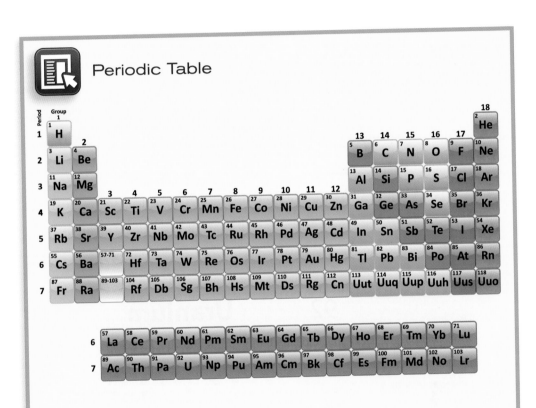

The Periodic Table of the Elements is arranged in numerical order. The number of each element is determined by the number of protons in its nucleus. The horizontal rows are called periods. The number of the elements increases across a period, from left to right. The vertical columns are called groups. Groups of elements share similar characteristics. The colors, which can vary depending on the way the creators design their version of the chart, also create related collections of elements, such as noble gases, metals, or nonmetals, among others.

in a few cases) three-letter symbol that represents the element. Most likely to be found: solid, liquid, or gas—based on its location. The periodic table is a very useful tool as one begins to investigate chemistry and science in general.

This book is about the element uranium. Uranium, the heaviest natural element on Earth, has 92 protons and 92 electrons. The most abundant isotope of uranium has 146 neutrons. Uranium is a silvery-white

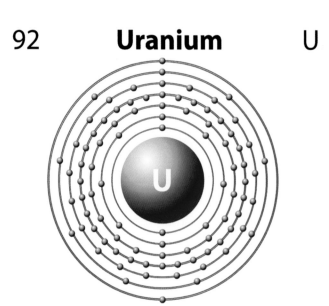

Uranium's nucleus is surrounded by a large cluster of 92 electrons arranged in seven orbital rings.

92   **Uranium**   U

Atomic mass: 238.02
Electron configuration: 2, 8, 18, 32, 21, 9, 2

metal that is found in minerals such as pitchblende. Uranium will tarnish when exposed to air, and if it is in the form of a very fine powder, it will ignite spontaneously. But what else makes this mineral unique?

Ask just about anyone about uranium and the first thing they will probably talk about is radioactivity. Uranium is a radioactive element, which breaks down into more stable elements while giving off energy. This energy has been used in weaponry and also to generate huge amounts of electricity. With its radioactive behavior and resulting products, uranium has many more uses and applications than those mentioned. Read on to find out more about how uranium is used in boats, as armor, as a way to determine the age of ancient rocks, and even to color glass. Find out how uranium deposits are found, how they are removed from the ground, and the special considerations that need to be taken in order to protect the environment and the people around the mineral. Plus, find out what the future holds for this fascinating element and natural resource.

U 92

Uranium

WORDS TO UNDERSTAND

depleted   reduced, eroded

fusion   when small nuclei combine to form a large nucleus, releasing energy

leaching   removing materials from solids by using water to rinse them out

ore   a naturally occurring mineral that exists in mineable quantities

phosphorescent   a material that absorbs radiation, in the form of light or electrons, and continues to emit light for a noticeable time after these emissions have stopped

proportional   existing in similar or like amounts

Discovery
and History

Uranium was discovered, in part, due to the silver mining industry in France. In the early 1500s, in a dense forest in France, miners discovered a huge deposit of silver. This was already one of the most valuable metals in the world, but this particular deposit held another treasure. This dig became the largest mining operation in Europe at the time and resulted in the production of more than two million silver coins. The region flourished, and silver became a worldwide form of currency.

There was a limited supply of silver in the mine, as with any natural resource. The supply lasted less than a century, and became **depleted**. Silver became cheaper and more economical to import from the American colonies than to continue mining

at this site. One hundred years after the mine prospered, it was nearly abandoned . . . but not closed. Deposits of bismuth and cobalt continued and, as technology and mining techniques improved, more silver was extracted from the mine. The miners also reported the presence of a shiny black mineral. They gave that black mineral the nickname "pitchblende" which means "bad luck mineral" in German.

The Element Gets a Name

In 1789, a German chemist named Martin Klaproth analyzed a sample of pitchblende. During his chemical experiments, he assumed the mineral was made of a pure element. He named the element "uranium." At a time when many of the newly discovered elements were named after the scientists who discovered them, Martin Klaproth took a different approach. Instead of potentially giving us the element "Klaprothium," he named his newly discovered element uranium. Uranium is named for the planet Uranus, which in turn, was named for Uranus the Greek God of the Sky. Uranus had been discovered in 1781. As it turned out, pitchblende is not pure uranium—it is a compound of uranium and oxygen, a mineral called uranium dioxide (UO_2).

Uranium takes its name from the planet Uranus, itself named for a Greek god.

In 1841, Klaproth's claim that pitchblende was pure uranium was discovered to be untrue. A French chemist named Eugene-Melchior Peligot became the first scientist to isolate pure uranium from a sample. He mixed uranium tetrachloride, UCl_4, with potassium. The uranium, a very dense element, can be separated from the other elements, although it was a difficult exercise. His findings helped further the scientific understanding of the mineral pitchblende.

While developing the periodic table in 1869, the Russian chemist and inventor Dmitry Mendeleev concluded that this new element, uranium, was the heaviest on Earth. Uranium has an atomic number of 92. All elements with higher atomic numbers are called transuranium

elements. These are only produced in a laboratory setting. They may have existed at one point in time on Earth, but are no longer found here. They most likely have decayed long ago into more stable elements.

One of the most significant properties of uranium wasn't discovered until 1896. At that time, a French physicist named Henri

Making Elements

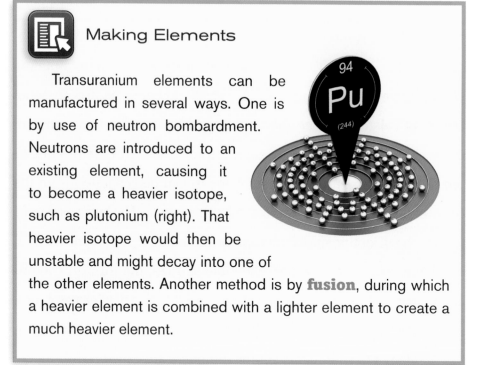

Transuranium elements can be manufactured in several ways. One is by use of neutron bombardment. Neutrons are introduced to an existing element, causing it to become a heavier isotope, such as plutonium (right). That heavier isotope would then be unstable and might decay into one of the other elements. Another method is by **fusion**, during which a heavier element is combined with a lighter element to create a much heavier element.

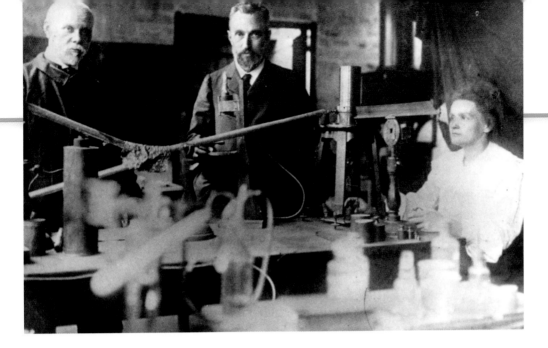

Luck helps: French scientist Henri Becquerel (center) got a little help from the sun.

Becquerel was conducting experiments to learn more about newly discovered X-rays. He was specifically looking at the way that a substance called uranyl potassium sulfate becomes **phosphorescent**, or glows, when exposed to the sun's light. During a stretch of cloudy weather, he left that paper and some uranium in a drawer. When he returned on a sunny day to continue his experiments, he found that the plate had fogged over, just like it did when it was placed in the sunshine. He concluded that the uranium compound in the drawer emitted rays that could have the same impact as the sun's radiation. In other words, uranium emitted rays undetectable under normal circumstances. These were later named Becquerel rays, or uranic rays.

Famed French scientist Marie Curie chose to study uranium and its rays as part of her doctoral thesis. She sought to accurately mea-

sure the rays emitted by uranium. Her initial results confirmed what Becquerel had discovered. That is, the amount of rays that a sample of uranium gave off was **proportional** to the concentration. In other words, the more uranium in a sample, the more rays were given off. Her studies found that a sample of pitchblende released more rays than she expected given the concentration of uranium in the mineral. Curie concluded that there must be other elements within the sample that also release rays. This led to the discovery of the elements polonium and radium. Ultimately, this led to the term "radiation," and her studies, along with those before her, confirmed that uranium is a radioactive element. It is weakly radioactive and breaks down, or decays, and releases the rays (or energy) over long periods of time.

This model shows how Marie Curie would have looked while at work in her lab.

Finding Uranium Today

At the present time, Kazakhstan, Canada, and Australia are the world's top three producers of uranium, contributing more than 60 percent of the entire world supply. Other countries contributing more than 1,000 tons (907 tonnes) of uranium each year include Niger, Namibia, Russia, China, the United States, Uzbekistan, and Malawi. Nearly all of the uranium mined today is used in nuclear power plants (see Chapter 4).

Finding deposits of uranium is made easier because uranium is radioactive. For years, the main tool for locating deposits of uranium was the Geiger counter. Geiger counters can detect alpha and beta particles as well as gamma rays. The counters detect the rays and emit clicking sounds or move needles on gauges to tell the operator where the uranium can be found. Other methods of exploration include airborne detectors that look for gamma rays emitted from the decay of uranium.

Uranium is mined in several ways. The method depends on the location and size of the deposit. Uranium is sometimes mined in more traditional open pit or underground mines. If the **ore** is near the

surface, an open pit method of mining where the overlying rock is removed may be employed. Large deposits that lie deep in the group may be removed with a subsurface or underground mine, requiring the miners to descend deep in the earth to remove the ore. Both of these methods can be expensive and present safety and health challenges to the environment and the miners.

An open-pit uranium mine in Australia

Another type of uranium mining operation involves drilling deep holes into a deposit. A chemical solution is pumped in through the hole to dissolve the ore, which is then pumped to the surface, where it can be processed. This method is frequently used when the available uranium ore deposit is relatively small. Sometimes, if the ore deposit doesn't contain a lot of uranium or it is of poor quality, a method called heap **leaching** is used. In this method, the ore is crushed and placed in piles that can be 15–90 feet (4.5–27 m) high. The pile sits for weeks, being rinsed with an acid solution. The liquid that

Meet the Curies

runs off the pile is collected and then treated to remove the uranium that leached into it.

Once removed from the earth, the uranium ore often needs to be processed to extract the usable uranium from the other minerals. Usually, sulfuric acid is used to remove the uranium. In any of the processes, the leftover material from the mining or the refining process must be dealt with very carefully. While the uranium that is being mined is not that dangerous as far as radioactivity is concerned, the elements from the radioactive decay of uranium are quite dangerous and hazardous to human health. Therefore, leftover uranium must be dealt with carefully so it doesn't harm the environment or the workers.

Uranium 92

Uranium miners are carefully monitored for exposure to the element's rays.

Workers are protected in a variety of ways. Ventilation standards within the subsurface mines are very high. This works to reduce the exposure to radon gas—a byproduct of the radioactive decay of uranium. The time that workers are exposed to the radiation is limited and regulated. In fact, in some mines in Canada, remote controls are used to work the equipment. Mines are closely monitored with radiation detection equipment. And the workers are trained, and retrained, as to the correct personal hygiene standards to reduce the transmission of potentially hazardous dust.

Uranium is a valuable and important material, but the people who mine for it are more valuable.

 Text-Dependent Questions

1. Who named uranium?

2. What scientist helped create the word "radiation"?

3. Name the top three uranium-producing countries in the world.

Research Project

Radon is an issue for family homes, too. Do some research on radon dectectors or alarms. Does your family have them? What does your local health department say about radon?

U 92
Uranium

WORDS TO UNDERSTAND

fission large nuclei split into smaller ones, releasing significant amounts of energy

plate tectonics a theory that describes the movement of Earth's tectonic plates

radioactive a property of some elements by which the unstable nucleus breaks down, or decays, into more stable elements

Chemical Properties

As we've seen, uranium is No. 92 on the periodic table. There are 92 protons in the nucleus of a uranium atom. The number of neutrons can vary; this is because there are many isotopes of this element. However, only two of those isotopes are stable. The rest can be made for only very brief periods of time.

Uranium is the heaviest naturally occurring element on Earth. All the elements that come after it on the periodic table have only been made in laboratories. Those heavier elements are **radioactive**. They are unstable atoms and release subatomic particles and energy as they break down to form more stable elements. This makes their existence on Earth difficult to monitor.

Uranium

A sample of Uranium 238 from Earth's beginning would only have decayed by half.

In most cases, uranium exists as a dense metal. This metal is typically silver to white in color and has a very high density. Uranium is actually one of the 10 densest metals on Earth. It is nearly twice as dense as lead, for example.

Uranium is radioactive as well. The reason, however that we find uranium on Earth has to do with its half-life. This measurement is a way to talk about the rate of decay of the element. The half-life of one isotope of uranium—Uranium–238—is about 4.5 billion years. This means that it takes 4.5 billion years for 50 percent (or half) of a sample of uranium to decay into some other stable element.

The age of the Earth is approximately 4.5 billion years. In other words, about half of all the uranium that ever formed on Earth is still around. This is why there is so much uranium on Earth. By comparison, element No. 93 on the periodic table—Neptunium—has a half-life of about two days.

Uranium's long half-life and radioactive properties have made it one of the most powerful elements on Earth. But, unlike silver or carbon, it is not used to make products. Instead, it is transformed and in changing, creates powerful energy that can be used.

Nuclear Fission

Nuclear **fission** is the splitting of an atom that releases a significant amount of energy. When nuclear fission occurs with uranium, the nucleus of an atom is split into smaller pieces. Typically, this happens when a stray neutron is captured by a larger nucleus, or it can occur spontaneously. Nuclear fission releases several different types of particles. This event generates a tremendous amount of energy. It also creates a chain reaction, in which the nuclei that are produced from the initial fission bombard and break apart

Nuclear fission and fusion

Uranium

other nuclei. That energy can be used in controlled ways, such as for nuclear power, or in uncontrolled uses, such as with a nuclear weapon.

To see how a chain reaction works, suppose that each Uranium–235 atom releases two neutrons during nuclear fission. Those two neutrons can then hit an additional two atoms of Uranium–238, releasing four more neutrons. Once that chain starts, it grows very quickly. Every 10 times it happens, there are 1,024 cases of nuclear fission occurring! Each time an atom of uranium-235 goes through fission it releases 200 million electron volts of energy. Doing the math shows that this chain reaction fission process can release a staggering amount of energy.

Uranium Inside Earth

Earth's interior is divided into layers. The inner layers—the mantle, outer core, and inner core—are a great source of heat for the planet. It is the radioactive decay of uranium, along with other elements—thorium and potassium—that supply the heat and energy. The heat in Earth's interior is responsible for surface processes such as **plate tectonics**. Plate tectonics shapes the surface of Earth, and

Albert Einstein and President Roosevelt

In 1939, German physicist Albert Einstein wrote a letter to President Franklin Delano Roosevelt discussing his research with uranium. Einstein and his team had been working on experiments involving fission chain reactions. They found that using uranium in the chain reactions created a great amount of power and that it might be possible to utilize that power to make a  very powerful and destructive bomb. Einstein believed that the Nazis in Germany were doing similar research into making this sort of weapon, and wrote to President Roosevelt to encourage him to do the same.

President Roosevelt took Einstein's concerns to heart. He soon formed the Advisory Committee on Uranium. This committee of scientists, civilians, and military personnel looked at the research being done on uranium at the time. Then they suggested how the US government should be involved. Eventually, this committee became part of the National Defense Research Committee. The scientific research began to focus on the fission chain reactions of uranium and its possible application toward building a bomb.

By the end of World War II, the United States had indeed created a bomb using this destructive power. Atomic bombs were dropped on two cities in Japan, Hiroshima and Nagasaki, in 1945.

the process of the movement of the plates is responsible for earthquakes, volcanoes, and mountain building.

It also impacts the interior of the Earth and Earth's movements. The temperatures in Earth's outer core are estimated to be between 7,200 and 9,000 °F (4,000°C to 5,000°C). These temperatures are enough to keep the iron and nickel in the outer core in a liquid state. The movement of this liquid metal in the outer core creates electric currents. Those currents are formed as warmer material rises inside the Earth and cooler material sinks. Add in the movement caused by the Earth's spin on its axis, and electricity is the result.

Intense heat inside the center of the Earth comes in part from uranium decay.

These electric currents in turn produce magnetic fields. The magnetic field reaches out from Earth's interior, into space, interacting with the charged particles coming off the Sun as part of the solar wind.

Geologists estimate that approximately 44 trillion watts of heat flow from Earth's interior out into space on a continual basis, in large part thanks to uranium.

 Text-Dependent Questions

1. What is the half-life of uranium−238?

2. To whom did Albert Einstein write concerning the potential of atomic weapons?

3. What is the difference between fission and fusion?

Research Project

Find a video that describes the geology at the core of the Earth. Make a poster showing the layers and indicate where uranium plays a part.

Uranium and You

Uranium has a bad reputation. Most people have heard of the element and are aware of the radioactive qualities of it. This has sparked both concern and misunderstanding about the element. It is true that uranium is radioactive and can be processed to create weapons. However, exposure to uranium in its raw form has been shown to be less problematic than one might think.

Even people who are not exposed to uranium in the workplace can be exposed. Uranium is often found naturally in drinking water. The concentrations vary from place to place but it is not uncommon for uranium to enter into a person's body through drinking water or a diet that includes root vegetables such as potatoes, beets, or carrots.

Once in the body, uranium is not easily absorbed into the digestive track. Most of the element is then passed from the body through urine. Extended exposure to uranium may lead to a buildup of the element in the kidneys, liver, and bones, although damage to the kidneys is of most concern.

The health effects of uranium exposure on miners working

in traditional uranium mines are fairly well known. Exposure to the actual uranium ore itself is relatively harmless—as long as it is not eaten and remains outside the body. However, during the mining process, especially when the ore is being extracted from an underground mine, those working the mine are exposed to fine dust particles. The particles can contain uranium and radon gas, both of which are known to cause cancers, especially lung cancers. Exposure to uranium dust and radon gas has also been linked to leukemia, stomach cancer, and birth defects.

While uranium itself may not be of great health concern to humans, one of the elements that forms as a result of its radioactive decay is of great concern. As we have seen, uranium is

radioactive. This means that, over time, atoms of uranium break down into other elements. Sometimes those elements are stable, other times they are themselves radioactive and continue to break down. Uranium is noteworthy because one of the elements that it breaks down to form during radioactive decay is radon. Radon, a gas on the periodic table with the atomic number of 86, is considered to be hazardous to human health.

Radon is colorless, tasteless, and odorless. Prolonged exposure to radon gas is the second leading cause of lung

cancer in the United States, after smoking tobacco products. People who smoke and are exposed to radon in their homes are even more likely to develop lung cancer. Radon can become concentrated in homes and offices, particularly in the lower floors or basements. Many areas of the country have high levels of radon—especially those that have bedrock rich in uranium. However, construction methods and can greatly influence the rate of radon seeping into homes and other buildings. Radon mitigation systems, which pump the air from beneath the basement or lower levels of a building up beyond the roof line where the radon gas mixes with the atmosphere and becomes less concentrated, are a relatively simple way to reduce exposure to this hazardous gas. And all new homes have to have monitors that can alert the residents if radon gas levels get too high.

U ^{92} **Uranium**

WORDS TO UNDERSTAND

compound two or more atoms chemically bonded

gaseous diffusion technology which forces a form of uranium through a membrane

Uranium Combines

Uranium is a metal. It will react with nearly all the non-metals on the periodic table to form **compounds**. Some of the more common uranium compounds are formed by bonds with oxygen, hydrogen, fluorine, or carbon.

One of the more common compounds that forms when uranium and oxygen combine is triuranium octoxide (U_3O_8). In fact, under most conditions this is the most stable form of uranium and is found in nature. Uranium dioxide (UO_2) is also common and is the form of uranium that is most frequently used as fuel in a nuclear reactor. Oxides of uranium are more stable than other forms of uranium and therefore are the form of uranium that is most likely to be stored or disposed of.

Uranium 92

There is a branch of science focused on the study of compounds containing carbon and uranium bonded together. This branch of chemistry had its origins during World War II under the Manhattan Project. This was the secret group of scientists and military personnel assembled by the United States to develop the atomic bomb. The project used uranium compounds for the separation of U–235 and U–238 isotopes. This type of chemistry has some importance in today's nuclear industry, too.

Uranium forms a compound with the element fluorine called uranium hexafluoride. A molecule with six atoms of fluorine and one atom of uranium, uranium hexafluoride serves an important role in the production of energy in a nuclear reactor. Uranium hexafluoride forms white crystals at room temperatures. It doesn't react with

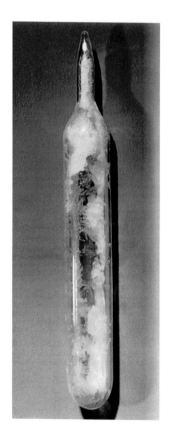

Uranium hexaflouride as crystals in a tube

The nuclear power industry—this is a plant control room—depends on uranium.

air, oxygen, or carbon dioxide. However, if it comes in contact with even the tiniest amount of water, it will react very quickly, mixing with the hydrogen and oxygen in water. It then gives off a new compound containing uranium, oxygen, and fluorine. The most troubling side effect of this reaction is that it also gives off the very toxic and corrosive acid HF, or hydrofluoric acid. For this reason, it is very important to keep samples of uranium hexafluoride away from water.

Uranium hexafluoride is used to separate the isotopes of uranium in a nuclear reactor. It is also used in the process to store depleted uranium. The vast majority of this depleted uranium is stored as uranium hexafluoride. It is then held in cylinders made of steel near the nuclear power plants where the enrichment procedure occurs. These

cylinders must be closely monitored for signs of wear, leaks, or corrosion to prevent the uranium hexafluoride from being exposed to water. In order to prevent the hazards of mixing with water, experts suggest that uranium hexafluoride be converted to a solid. This process, however, would cost millions of dollars and has thus far proven to be too expensive to undertake on a large scale.

When heated, uranium isotope deuterium glows a rosy red.

Uranium also forms compounds with the different isotopes of hydrogen. One of the most common compounds is uranium hydride, which consists of one atom of uranium and three atoms of the hydrogen isotope deuterium. When a sample of uranium metal is heated to moderately high temperatures, it reacts with hydrogen to form uranium hydride. Further heating removes the hydrogen. This is a useful property, especially when making a uranium powder that can be used for nuclear fuel. Uranium hydride can also be produced when uranium metal is exposed to water or steam.

The team of scientists who worked on the atomic bomb in the 1930s created an alternative design for the device that used uranium hydride. This bomb used deuterium, an isotope of hydrogen with one proton and one neutron. When deuterium reacts with uranium, there is a very slow chain reaction. This proved to be less effective in a bomb because the fission reaction was so slow. Two uranium hydride bombs were tested but they only produced the equivalent of 200 tons of TNT each. This was not enough energy so scientists then looked for other compounds that used faster reaction rates to make the atomic bombs.

Uranium

Nuclear Weapons

While uranium does combine with other elements to form compounds, it is the element's radioactive properties that have the most impact on society and on the health of the environment and living things. One of the most significant uses of that explosive and radioac-

The US lab at Oak Ridge continues as an energy research facility today.

∷rails

TO:

CHVY

Code or full name of library

FOR:

_____

_____

Code or full name of destination library

FROM:

WOLY

NOTES / DATE DUE:

_____

tive power is in the destructive blasts of nuclear weapons.

As you read earlier, Albert Einstein encouraged President Franklin Roosevelt to investigate the radioactive properties of uranium in the pursuit of an atomic bomb. The president

The Manhattan Project

appointed a committee to investigate the matter, and the Manhattan Project was born. Research into using uranium was already in the works, but it was the mission of the Manhattan Project to speed up that research and investigate the possible applications.

Scientists recognized early on that one of the first challenges that needed to be overcome was the enriching of the uranium. This process helped make sure there would be enough of the necessary U–235 for use. The process to make this isotope takes a huge amount of work. To create the U–235, an enrichment laboratory was built in Oak Ridge, Tennessee. There, different methods were tried. One used **gaseous diffusion** to extract the uranium. Another used magnetics to separate the isotopes of uranium from each other. Once the

isotopes were fully separated, all that needed to be done was to initiate the fission reaction.

Robert Oppenheimer (below and also pictured on page 36 with Gen. Leslie Groves) was the director of the Manhattan Project in 1942. He recommended that the project be moved from Tennessee to Los Alamos, New Mexico. Due to the sensitivity of the project and the potential health and environmental dangers of enriching uranium, he thought that moving the project to a more remote area would be a prudent idea.

Research continued until December 1942

A brilliant physicist, Robert Oppenheimer was the director of the Manhattan Project.

when Enrico Fermi, at the University of Chicago, conducted the very first nuclear chain reaction. Finally, with this advance in controlling nuclear fission, it was possible to build, and control, an atomic bomb.

 Text-Dependent Questions

1. Why do uranium hexaflouride and water make a bad combination?

2. In what state was uranium refined for use in the Manhattan Project?

3. What isotope of hydrogen was tried in a bomb first?

Research Project

Oppenheimer later came to regret some of the work his team did. He famously said, "I am become death, the destroyer of worlds." Read more about him online and find out where that quote came from and what he meant by it.

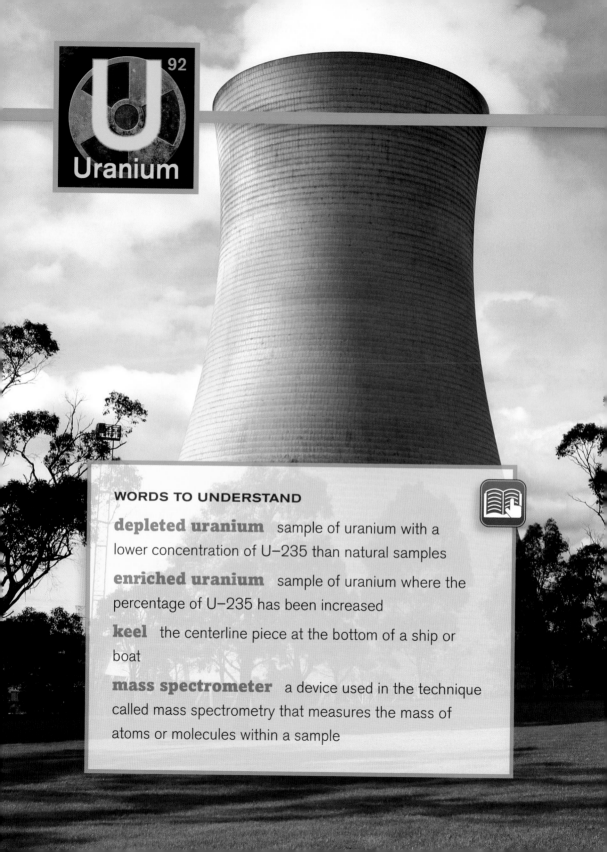

U 92 Uranium

WORDS TO UNDERSTAND

depleted uranium   sample of uranium with a lower concentration of U−235 than natural samples

enriched uranium   sample of uranium where the percentage of U−235 has been increased

keel   the centerline piece at the bottom of a ship or boat

mass spectrometer   a device used in the technique called mass spectrometry that measures the mass of atoms or molecules within a sample

Uranium in Our World

One of the most well-known and significant uses of uranium is as a source of fuel. As we've seen, uranium is also a main source of material for nuclear weapons. However, there are other uses for uranium in a variety of different forms.

Radiometric Dating Techniques

The radioactive behavior of uranium and its daughter products, coupled with its very long half-life, makes uranium an excellent tool in determining the age of geologic samples. Geologic samples that are at least one million years old, that is.

Formally, it is the uranium-lead method of dating, as scientists look at the decay of U–238 to Pb–206 or U–235 to

Pb–207. Geologists take a sample of a rock and remove small samples of the mineral zircon from it. Zircon ($ZrSiO4$) is a very hard mineral that often has impurities containing uranium. These facts make zircon a very useful mineral when it comes to determining the age of the rock in which it is found. Zircon doesn't break down until it is exposed to

Working parts of a mass spectrometer in a laboratory setting

temperatures greater than 900°C. This means that the processes that form igneous, metamorphic, and sedimentary rocks may not reset that zircon. The zircon will remain largely unchanged from the time it forms. Therefore, scientists can look at the ratio of uranium

Nuclear power debate

to lead in the sample and calculate a very accurate age of the mineral.

Zircon is widespread in many igneous rocks. It is easily separated from the rest of the rock due to its high density. Techniques of crushing a rock sample and then filtering out the zircon using acids and other chemicals allow scientists to obtain the samples needed for U–Pb analysis.

Analysis is completed in a device called a **mass spectrometer**. In this case, the zircon sample is placed within a magnetic field. The atoms of zircon are ionized, and then the ions are accelerated. These accelerated ions are deflected by the magnetic field within the mass spectrometer and separated based on their mass. The different masses reflect the different isotopes of uranium and lead that are present

This complicated nuclear power plant control room is in Russia.

in the zircon sample. The isotopes are then detected and analyzed for their relative amounts. Mathematical calculations are used to determine the ratio between the parent and the daughter material. Using the known half-life of the parent material (in this case uranium) and that ratio, an age of the rock can be calculated. Uranium-lead dating techniques are precise within the 0.1–1.0% range.

Nuclear Reactors

A nuclear power plant is fundamentally the same as a power plant that uses fossil fuels. In both cases, there must be a source of heat. The heat is used to generate steam, which drives the turbines and, ultimately, the generators that make the energy that is used by thousands. A nuclear power plant uses uranium and fission reactions to make this happen, instead of burning coal or other fossil fuels. This necessitated an ability to control the fission chain reaction of uranium atoms and—specifically—the fission chain reaction of Uranium–235.

When U–235 decays, it releases two alpha particles (2 protons and 2 neutrons) along with energy. However when uranium is mined, it is about 99.3 percent U–238 and only about 0.7 percent U-235. In order

The Chemistry of Everyday Elements

Uranium 92

to get enough U–235 to use in a nuclear reactor, the uranium must be enriched. The goal is to concentrate the U–235 in a sample to a level of about 5 percent. This is done through a process known as gaseous diffusion. The uranium is turned into a gas and passed through a permeable membrane. As this happens, the isotopes are separated from each other. The U–238 is now considered to be **depleted uranium** and can be applied to other uses.

The **enriched uranium** is then shaped into pellets, about one inch long and with the diameter of a dime. These pellets are arranged into rods and then bundled together. The bundles are placed in a pressurized water container that provides cooling. Without this cooling mechanism, the uranium, as it undergoes the fission reaction, would become very hot and melt.

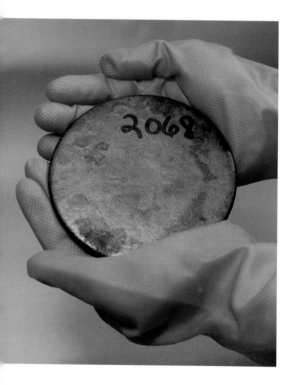

An enriched uranium disk

The tubes at right are where the all-important control rods go in a reactor.

As an additional check to make sure this doesn't happen, control rods are used. Control rods are made to absorb neutrons and can be lowered into or raised out of the bundles of enriched uranium. This allows the rate of the nuclear reaction to be controlled. To increase the rate of the fission reactions, the control rods are raised out of the bundle, and, therefore, the neutrons are passed into the enriched uranium rods. To slow down the reaction, and thus decrease the amount of heat in the system, the control rods are moved down into the bundles.

The uranium bundles create a staggering amount of heat as nuclear fission is allowed to happen. The heat changes the water to steam. This steam then drives a turbine, which produces electrical power in a generator.

When those control rods fail, however, there might be terrible consequences. The most recent and well-known such nuclear plant

breakdown came in 2011 after an earthquake caused a tsunami to strike the eastern coast of Japan. One of the buildings hit by the wave was the Fukushima power plant. When seawater rushed in, the plant was not able to function properly. For a time, the control rods were not able to do their job. The tsunami disrupted the power supply and the superheated water could not be cooled down. Plant engineers had

Fukushima residents had to be scanned for radiation after visiting their homes.

Uranium Supplies

At present, the world consumption of uranium is roughly 66 kilotons per year. Nearly all that uranium is used in the nuclear power industry. Initially, between 1945 and 1958, uranium was primarily used for military applications. In the 1970s, there was a lot of interest in exploring and using uranium for power but that waned until 2003 or so when exploration efforts increased as the renewed interest in nuclear power came to the forefront. This increase in exploration efforts has driven the cost of uranium ore. Exploration has driven up the costs of uranium ore, and it appears as if this trend will continue.

Experts estimate that at the current rate of usage, the supply of uranium mined on the surface or subsurface of Earth will last another 200 years. There are approximately 5.5 million tons of known uranium reserves with roughly 10.5 million tons undiscovered. These numbers will change as better exploration and mining techniques are developed.

The Chemistry of Everyday Elements

to release radioactive water and air to prevent an explosion. Officials ordered a massive evacuation so that exposure would be limited. People up to 12.5 miles (20 km) from the plant had to leave their homes. Still, the dangerous air and water was out there. Even more than five years later, scientists are still finding its effects in the ocean water.

Fukushima was a minor accident compared to one in Chernobyl, Russia, in 1986. A series of errors by plant operators caused an explosion and a massive release of radiation. Even today, most of the area around the plant is not safe for humans to live in. More than 300,000 people had to be moved to new homes. They saw a huge rise in the number of cancer cases, almost certainly linked to the radiation released during the explosion and fire. Incidents such as Fukushima and Chernobyl play a big part in the ongoing safety debate.

Depleted Uranium in Action

The uranium enrichment process creates depleted uranium—a byproduct with 0.3 percent or less U–235. This uranium product, often abbreviated DU, is very dense and weakly radioactive. Recall that the half-life of U–238 is about 4.5 billion years. An element's biological

An abandoned amusement park in Chernobyl remains as a reminder of a disaster.

half-life is the amount of time for 50 percent of the uranium in the body to be eliminated. For DU, this is about 15 days. So that means if it gets into a person's body, it is there for more than two weeks, potentially causing harm. As a result, the use of depleted uranium is controversial.

Even with this danger, DU is used for many applications. Very dense DU is often used in the **keels** of boats or as a counterweight in aircraft. It has been used as shields in medical radiation applications, and to line the containers used to ship other, more radioactive materials. The military, in the US and in other countries, uses DU as armor plating in vehicles and to make projectiles that can then pierce a similar armor plate.

Uranium 92

Glass

Uranium is used as an additive to glassware to produce distinctive colors. Uranium glass, or Vaseline glass as it is sometimes referred to, is typically yellow or green. The actual color depends on the concentrations of uranium in the glass. Uranium glass will fluoresce, or glow, a bright green color when placed in ultraviolet light.

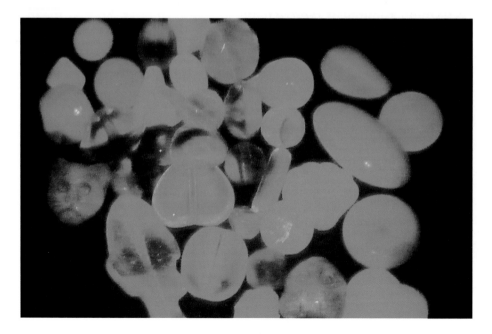

Treated with uranium, bits of glass will glow with an eerie green light.

A Geiger counter reads the levels of radiation given off by uranium.

Some samples of uranium glass will register on a Geiger counter, indicating that they are radioactive. For the most part, the samples are harmless to humans and release very small amounts of radioactivity.

The use of uranium to color glass has been around since at least the year 79. Yellow glass was found in Italy by archeologists from England in the early 1900s. The glass was very popular in the 1880s, too. Uranium glass was produced in the United States until World War II, when the government took over the supplies of uranium for other uses.

Uranium From Seawater

It is estimated that there are roughly 4.5 billion metric tons of uranium in the world's oceans. It is, however, at a concentration of just over three parts per billion. Scientists are working on technologies that would allow for the extraction of usable uranium from seawater. It has been an idea that has been explored in the past, but the technol-

Uranium

ogy just wasn't there to make the procedure worthwhile. Technology involving a polymer, a material very much like plastic, has been developed that might make extracting that uranium pay off. The polymer is made into long braids and taken by boat to the ocean. The braids are lowered to a depth of about 300 feet (91 m) where they are chained to the ocean floor and allowed to float freely for about two months. They are then removed from the ocean floor, at times appearing yellow due to the accumulated uranium, and taken back to a facility where the uranium is removed with a solvent. Overall, about two to four grams of uranium per kilogram of polymer can be collected this way.

This may not sound like a lot, but as Erich Schneider, a nuclear engineer at the University of Texas at Austin, points out, "It all adds up." At the moment, scientists admit this is not a method that will replace traditional mining efforts. But it is possible to be used as a backup. And as the technology improves and more and more uranium can be extracted using this polymer method, it is possible that one day the vast amount of uranium in the ocean could be used on a larger scale.

Uranium is an important and prominent metal element. Its radioactivity makes it a bit scary, yes, but it can be harnessed to help hu-

Is the ocean the next source of uranium? Scientists are working on the answer.

mans by providing power, which might be a significant help in the future if enough safety procedures can be put in place. That could then create a lot of good in the world . . . assuming, of course, that we don't use the massive energy of uranium to blow each other up first.

 Text-Dependent Questions

1. What do control rods do in a nuclear power plant?

2. When was the Chernobyl disaster?

3. What does the US military use depleted uranium for?

Research Project

Read more about both sides of the nuclear power debate. Prepare a pro and con debate list with facts to support each side.

FIND OUT MORE

Books

Sheinkin, Steve. ***Bomb: The Race to Build—and Steal—the World's Most Dangerous Weapon.*** New York, NY: Flashpoint, 2012. The use of uranium to make a very dangerous weapon became a race against time. Read all about it here.

Venezia, Mike. ***Marie Curie: Scientist Who Made Glowing Discoveries.*** New York, NY: Black Dog & Leventhal, 2012. Find out more about the life and work of Marie Curie in this book.

Zoellner, Tom. ***Uranium: War, Energy, and the Rock That Shaped the World.*** New York, NY: Penguin, 2009. Are you interested in the history behind the use of uranium in World War II and after? Read this book to find out more.

Web Sites

science.howstuffworks.com/nuclear-power2.htm
Exactly how does a nuclear power plant work? Find out on this site.

www.atomicarchive.com/Docs/Begin/Einstein.shtml
Read for yourself the letters that Albert Einstein sent to President Roosevelt.

geoinfo.nmt.edu/resources/uranium/mining.html
Uranium can be mined in several different ways. Learn more about the pros and cons of each method on this site.

SERIES GLOSSARY OF KEY TERMS

carbohydrates a group of organic compounds including sugars, starches, and fiber

conductivity the ability of a substance for heat or electricity to pass through it

inert unable to bond with other matter

ion an atom with an electrical charge due to the loss or gain of an electron

isotope an atom of a specific element that has a different number of neutrons; it has the same atomic number but a different mass

nuclear fission process by which a nucleus is split into smaller parts releasing massive amounts of energy

nuclear fusion process by which two atomic nuclei combine to form a heavier element while releasing energy

organic compound a chemical compound in which one or more atoms of carbon are linked to atoms of other elements (most commonly hydrogen, oxygen, or nitrogen)

spectrum the range of electromagnetic radiation with respect to its wavelength or frequency; can sometimes be observed by characteristic colors or light

solubility the ability of a substance to dissolve in a liquid

Uranium

INDEX

Photo Credits

Dreamstime.com: Reinout van Wagtendonk 7, snapgalleria 8, Blueringmedia 10, carolecastelli 12, conceptTW 16, Johncarnemolla 20, Darko Hristov 22, Vladivitek24, 55, Antony Mcaulay 26, Leonello Calvetti 30, Scott Prokop 33, Robert Gubiani 46, Dreamstimepoint 48, Pozitivstudija 50, calflier110 57, Sergiy Gaydaenko 59, Wrangel 61. Library of Congress: 29, 44. NASA: 15. Newscom: Keizo Mori/UPI 54. Shutterstock: Radiokafka 53. US Army: 36. US Department of Energy: 38, 42, 52. Carl Willis Project: 39. Wikimedia: 17, 18, BenCBartlett 40, Wombat1138 58.

About the Author

Jane P. Gardner has written more than 30 books for young and young-adult readers on science and other nonfiction topics. She authored the *Science 24/7* series as well as several titles in the *Black Achievements in Science* series. In addition to her writing career, she also has years of classroom teaching experience. Jane taught middle school and high school science and currently teaches chemistry at North Shore Community College in Massachusetts. She lives in eastern Massachusetts with her husband and two sons.